W9-BLM-799

Authors
Kids Love

Sid Fleischman

An Author Kids Love

New Postage Rates

by Michelle Parker-Rock

Enslow Elementary

an imprint of

Enslow Publishers, Inc.

40 Industrial Road
Box 398
Berkeley Heights, NJ 07922
USA

http://www.enslow.com

This book is based on a live interview with Sid Fleischman on February 21, 2006.

For my father, a vaudevillian at heart. And for S.F., respectfully. Thanks.

Copyright © 2009 by Michelle Parker-Rock

All rights reserved.

No part of this book may be reproduced by any means without the written permission of the publisher.

Library of Congress Cataloging-in-Publication Data

Parker-Rock, Michelle.

Sid Fleischman : an author kids love / Michelle Parker-Rock.

p. cm. — (Authors kids love)

"Based on a live interview with Sid Fleischman on February 21, 2006"—T.p. verso.

Summary: "Discusses the life of children's author Sid Fleischman, including his childhood, writing career, and his advice for young writers"—Provided by publisher.

Includes index.

ISBN-13: 978-0-7660-2757-2

ISBN-10: 0-7660-2757-0

1. Fleischman, Sid, 1920–   —Juvenile literature. 2. Fleischman, Sid, 1920–   —Interviews—Juvenile literature. 3. Authors, American—20th century—Biography—Juvenile literature. 4. Authors, American—20th century—Interviews—Juvenile literature. 5. Children's stories—Authorship—Juvenile literature. I. Title.

PS3556.L42269Z462 2008

813'.54—dc22

[B]

2007046079

Printed in the United States of America

To Our Readers: We have done our best to make sure that all Internet Addresses in this book were active and appropriate when we went to press. However, the author and publisher have no control over and assume no liability for the material available on those Internet sites or on other Web sites they may link to. Any comments or suggestions can be sent by e-mail to comments@enslow.com or to the address on the back cover.

♻ Enslow Publishers, Inc., is committed to printing our books on recycled paper. The paper in every book contains 10% to 30% post-consumer waste (PCW). The cover board on the outside of each book contains 100% PCW. Our goal is to do our part to help young people and the environment too!

Photo Credits: Courtesy of Sid Fleischman, pp. 3, 6, 9, 15, 16, 17, 19, 21, 22, 24, 25, 27, 33, 44, 47, back cover; Library of Congress, p. 35; Kevin O'Malley, pp. 1, 42; Michelle Parker-Rock © 2006, pp. 4, 39, 40; Shutterstock, p. 12.

Cover Photo: Kevin O'Malley.

Contents

Chapter 1   Taking Chances 5

Chapter 2   Abracadabra 8

Chapter 3   Hocus Pocus 14

Chapter 4   Presto Chango 20

Chapter 5   Mr. Mysterious 31

Chapter 6   Practice and Persistence 38

BOOKS   by Sid Fleischman 45

Words to Know 46

Further Reading and Internet Addresses .. 47

Index 48

Taking Chances

Sid Fleischman was taking a shower one morning in January 1987 when the phone rang. His wife, Betty, took the message. She told him it was a call from a woman in Chicago. Minutes later, Fleischman returned the call. He discovered that he had won the most distinguished award in children's literature, the Newbery Medal, for his novel *The Whipping Boy*. Fleischman was ecstatic.

Years earlier, he had come across the idea for the book while doing research for another writing project. He read about a historical practice where young boys and girls who lived in royal households took the punishment for the wrongdoings of the

Fleischman wearing the Newbery Medal he won for *The Whipping Boy*. The Newbery is one of the most prestigious awards in children's literature.

princes and princesses. Fleischman took a chance and set out to write a tale about two young boys— one, the spoiled Prince Brat, and the other, an orphan named Jemmy. Jemmy is kept in the castle to take the blame for Prince Brat's bad behavior.

At first, Fleischman thought it would be a brief story.

"I told myself that it was a picture book," he said. He was slow to see that his original concept for the book was wrong. The problem facing Fleischman was that a picture book manuscript is usually only a few pages long. "It was taking me five pages just to set the story up," he said. "I kept trying to cut it and that wasn't working either."

Fleischman struggled with the story for almost ten years, finally giving it one last chance. "I wrote

many other books during this ten-year period," he said, "but this tale kept nagging at me. It was only when I relaxed," he said, "that I finally let the story surprise me and write itself."

He said:

> As a writer, one thing you learn early on is you can't give up. If you give up you never succeed at all. There are always problems to face. You have to persist. If you don't persist, your game is finished.

For Fleischman, taking chances and persevering were nothing new. In fact, they were two things he did well, even as a young boy.

Max Brindle

Fleischman also wrote the screenplay for the movie version of *The Whipping Boy*. All was going well until the producers decided to make a key change to the story. Fleischman thought the change did not make sense, so he took his own name off the screenplay and used a pen name. He chose "Max Brindle," the name of the detective in his first adult novel. The movie got excellent reviews, but the credit went to the fictional hero, Brindle. Fleischman was amused.

Chapter 2

Abracadabra

It was a fall day in 1929 when a traveling show came to downtown San Diego and moved into an empty storefront on Fifth Avenue. There were many empty shops that year. It was the beginning of the Great Depression, a time when millions of people lost their jobs and homes.

Fortunately for the young Sid Fleischman, his parents were able to provide for their family. His father, Reuben, a Jewish immigrant, had come to the United States from Russia in 1908. He settled in New York, where he worked in sweatshop factories and drove a taxi. He married Sadie, the daughter of Jewish immigrants, and the couple settled in Brooklyn.

The Fleischmans had three children: Pearl, born in 1918; Albert Sidney, born on March 16, 1920; and Arleen, born eight years later. Reuben and Sadie gave their son the Jewish name Avrom Zalmon, which they changed to the more American-sounding Albert Sidney. However, they called him Sonny Boy until he complained. Then he became Sid. It was not until he was about seven or eight that Sid found out his first name was Albert.

Reuben Fleischman was a man who took chances. Sid Fleischman said:

My father was an immigrant from the Ukraine, a little town called Olyk. He was the oldest of five kids. He came over with his father when he was about sixteen, and then his father died. As the oldest, he became the bread ticket for the rest of his family. He was a skilled tailor, and little by little, he saved enough to bring his mother

Sid with his parents and older sister, Pearl, in 1923.

and his brothers and sisters over. He left the sweatshops and he actually managed to buy a taxicab. Later, he was embarrassed about that. He never wanted to talk about the fact that he had driven a cab. I remember seeing pictures of him with a billed taxi cap. Then he opened a store that sold ribbons and stuff used in tailoring. My mother was about eighteen or nineteen when they met. She was born in Brooklyn. Her parents came from England. Further back, they, too, had come from Russia. She was one of ten kids.

Fleischman's father took another risk by going to California in 1922.

He took a chance that he would find something and he did. He decided this is where he would try to put down roots. Then he sent for my mother, my oldest sister, and me. When my mother came to California, she was isolated for the first few years. Then one by one, members of her family came out. Pretty soon they were all here.

Because Reuben Fleischman was a tailor, he could generally make a living anywhere. He started a business in San Diego as a naval tailor because it was a big navy town.

The sideshow troupe that moved into the vacant space next door to Reuben Fleischman's shop on Fifth Avenue in downtown San Diego featured a group of traveling performers. The show caught the attention of nine-year-old Sid.

"You paid about five cents to get in and then saw all these acts. They called it a 'Ten in One.' Ten acts for one price."

Sid went to see the performers.

"They had a sharpshooter and a ventriloquist and a fat lady and a magician," he said. Later on, when he wrote *Jim Ugly*, a show business story about a boy and his dog set in the Wild West, he used the memories of the sideshow to create characters like the world-famous sharpshooter and actress Miss Jenny, the Arizona Girl.

Fleischman's father became acquainted with the owner of the troupe, so eventually Sid went in without paying. It was there that he met his first magician.

"Fortunately for me he was a very, very skilled magician," said Fleischman. "He, too, had fallen on hard times, and he ended up in this carnival."

Sideshow performers—
an acrobat, juggler, and
tattooed man—in the
early twentieth century.

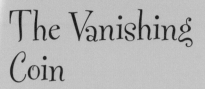

Sid was enchanted by the conjurer's act, and he was amazed by what the wizard could do. He said:

I'd keep going back to watch this magician and pretty soon I got to know him. He'd send me on errands. I'd be delighted to run to the print shop and get some paper or whatever he needed. He showed me my first trick and how to do it. I still occasionally perform it. It was a vanishing coin trick. It really set me in magic cement, and I still have my feet stuck in it.

The Vanishing Coin

This trick is what a magician calls sleight of hand, which means "skill with the hands," especially in fooling onlookers. To do the trick you need a coin. Hold it between the tips of your thumb and index finger on your left hand. Move your right hand over your left hand making it look like you are grabbing the coin. Instead, let the coin fall into the base of the fingers of your left hand. Quickly close your right hand as if the coin were inside it, and take the hand away. Say a magic word or blow on your right hand. Then slowly open your right fingers to show that the coin has vanished. Magicians call this trick "the French Drop."

Chapter 3

Hocus Pocus

"**I** have happy memories of growing up," said Fleischman.

I shouldn't have because they were tough times. During the Depression, we knew that things were bad, but there was always food on the table and a roof over our heads. But if we needed money, we really had to work on our father. We didn't realize what he was going through.

Despite the times, Fleischman had a full childhood. He played the clarinet in the school orchestra and read *Huckleberry Finn* and *Robin Hood*.

"We had the beach," he said, "and summers were marvelous."

Fleischman also listened to the radio, and he especially enjoyed a daily program starring Chandu the Magician, a character that fought evil with his magic powers. Fleischman dreamed about becoming a famous magician himself. He said:

> Of course, the problem was how I could learn to be a magician, particularly at that age. There were no magic shops in San Diego and no one gave lessons that I knew of. I did have the good sense to go to the library to see if there was a book or two on magic, and there was. I taught myself my first magic tricks out of library books.

Fleischman says he was a happy child. He was about three years old when this photo was taken.

His father was upset. "He thought I was wasting my time and that I would starve to death as a magician. He was probably right."

Fleischman treasured his collection of paperback

Sid with Pearl, his
older sister.

magic books and a small box of props and gadgets. He said:

With the best of intentions, parents can sometimes do the cruelest things. I came home from school one day, and all my magic was gone. My little tricks and gimmicks were gone. My mother wasn't home so I went looking for them in the trash barrel, where I found everything neatly stacked. I was furious. When my mother came back, she said that my dad insisted that she throw away my stuff because I had no future as a magician. Nevertheless, she let me keep the trick props. I think the episode was just a dramatic way to let me know that dad was not happy with my choice of careers and that I better find something else a little more practical.

Although Fleischman understood his father's

16

concerns, he persisted. He just kept his magic to himself for a while.

"Dad wanted me to be able to make a living," said Fleischman. "He was actually right. It's very hard to make a living in any of the arts, if you include magic as one of the arts."

At the age of thirteen, Fleischman had a bar mitzvah, a religious Jewish ceremony that marked his transition into manhood. He said:

The bar mitzvah may have declared me to be a man, and I may have believed it for the weekend. But on Monday, I returned to junior high school—a kid in corduroys again. It was only years later that I came to understand how profoundly affected I was to be accepted by that ceremony into the courageous 5,000-year-old history of the Jewish people.

Sid and his father on a California beach. Reuben Fleischman did not understand his son's interest in magic.

While he began to take life more seriously, Fleischman was also discovering that the world had a sense of humor. Decades later, this informed his literary style.

> At age fifteen, a momentous moment came along when somebody I knew said he had seen something in the newspaper about a magic club in San Diego. He cut it out and gave it to me. The club meetings were held in a real estate office not far from where we lived.

The president of the group was Charles W. Fait, also known as Professor Fait the Great.

"He had been a traveling magician," Fleischman recalled. "I can remember the scent of this man and his cigar smoke."

Fleischman was eager to sign up, but Professor Fait had doubts. As Fleischman tells it:

> He said, "We don't have kids in the club, but let me think about it." Then he asked me to do a little something. I performed a few sleight-of-hand things, and he realized that I was really serious. So, he said, "Ok, you can join." Of course, that was just nirvana. So every month I would work up some magic trick that I could do for the members

Professor Fait in his early days as a traveling magician. In this trick, he has shuffled selected cards into a deck, thrown the deck into the air, and then impaled the selected cards on a sword.

of the club. Some had been professional magicians or semiprofessional, but they were all skilled in magic. The experience was a huge step forward for me. After that, I never looked back. I would become a magician.

Presto Chango

Chapter 4

All through high school, Fleischman was known as the kid who did magic.

"It was great," he said. "I used to read palms, because then you could hold the girls' hands. I made up all the fortune-telling. Everyone does."

At Professor Fait's Magician's Club of San Diego, Fleischman met his pal Buddy Ryan. The two teens became fast friends and partners in magic. The Mirthful Conjurers, as they called themselves, kept busy doing magic shows around town. Then during the summer of 1936, when Fleischman was sixteen and Ryan was seventeen, they took their new show, See'n Is Believ'n, on the road and up through the

Sierra Nevada mountains. Although he did not know it at the time, Fleischman's experiences in the gold country of California would later turn up in several of his novels for young readers.

"By the time I got out of high school, my dream was to get into vaudeville," Fleischman said. Vaudeville was a kind of staged variety show popular in the first part of the twentieth century.

> Instead of going on to college, I went to Los Angeles and registered with a booking agent to do tours. Then in due time, I got a job in a magic show, traveling all over the country, which I did for two years.

While still in high school, Fleischman wrote his first book, entitled *Between Cocktails*. It explained tricks that can be done with paper matches.

In this photo, Sid Fleischman is fifteen years old. He became known for his skill at magic.

Sid Fleischman (right) with Buddy Ryan and the poster advertising their magic act.

"With that title, I was trying to be very sophisticated," he said.

The world of conjuring was very small in those days. There were just a few publishers of magic books. Fleischman sent his manuscript to one of those publishers, who bought the rights to publish it for fifty dollars.

"I was delighted," said Fleischman.

It was exciting for him to see his name in print. He wanted to write and publish more. He admired the works of O. Henry and Guy de Maupassant, whose stories, like his own magic tricks, had surprise endings. But his early efforts at writing short fiction garnered nothing but rejection slips.

"The harder I tried, the more I enjoyed the

challenge of coming up with fresh stories that read well," Fleischman said.

To improve his skills, Fleischman decided to go to college. To help pay for his tuition, he started his own magic company.

"It was called The Little Shop of Hocus Pocus," he said. "It was a card table in my bedroom. Boy, was it small. Most of the time, I wasn't even there. I was traveling."

Fleischman made it work by advertising his tricks in popular magic journals.

> My mother handled things for me. I would send her all the stuff I made up. Almost everything sold for a dollar, which was about as much as most magicians could afford in those days for gimmicks and tricks. When my father saw these dollar bills coming in through the mail, he was a little more impressed.

Fleischman explained how his business worked:

> I was selling original tricks. I sent instructions and some gimmick that went with it. I'd send those to my mother, who would fill the orders as they came in and hold the money for my college expenses to

come. My tricks were very good. Some of them are still being performed all over the country.

After Fleischman quit the show, he enrolled in San Diego State College, now San Diego State University. The income from his business plus the money he earned performing magic at local nightclubs paid for his schoolbooks and other expenses.

"I was an English major," said Fleischman. "By that time, I was sure that I wanted to become a writer."

The business card and handbill for Buddy and Sid, who called themselves "The Mirthful Conjurers."

Fleischman took a course in writing short stories. One of his teachers, John Adams, was very helpful. He taught Fleischman how to appreciate literature and encouraged him to write.

During this time, another big event occurred in Fleischman's life. He met his future wife, Betty Taylor. Then World War II came around, and he went into the naval reserve. Fleischman trained in the military part-time in preparation for active duty in an emergency. He was assigned clerical work because he was a good typist. In 1942, he married Betty. Soon after, the Navy transferred him to a naval recruiting office in New York City, and the couple moved east.

Fleischman excelled at card tricks.

Fleischman continued to write. When the good news came that he had sold a story to *Liberty*, a popular magazine of the day, he felt like his ship had come in. It was his big break. He finally saw himself as a fiction writer.

Later that year, Fleischman received orders to leave on the USS *Albert T. Harris*, a destroyer that sailed with supply ships to protect them in enemy waters. He spent four years in the Navy, mostly in the Far East. While at sea, Fleischman edited the ship's newspaper and wrote more stories.

After the war, the couple moved back to San Diego, and Fleischman decided not to return to college immediately. Instead, he wrote full-time in hopes of making enough money to pay the bills. He experienced some rejections and some sales. Encouraged, he decided to write a novel for adults. It starred detective Max Brindle. *The Straw Donkey Case* was published in 1948, and that same year, Fleischman sold a sequel. The novels earned little money.

He went back to college, taking advantage of funds the government provided for people who had served in the military. In 1949, Fleischman graduated with a bachelor's degree in English.

"Now, I'm out of college and turned loose on the world," he said. "I was still giving magic shows. I was working nightclubs for thirty-five dollars a week, so I was able to pay my bills."

Fleischman took a job as a journalist for the *San Diego Daily Journal*. He liked being in the newspaper business. "I think I was a good reporter," he said.

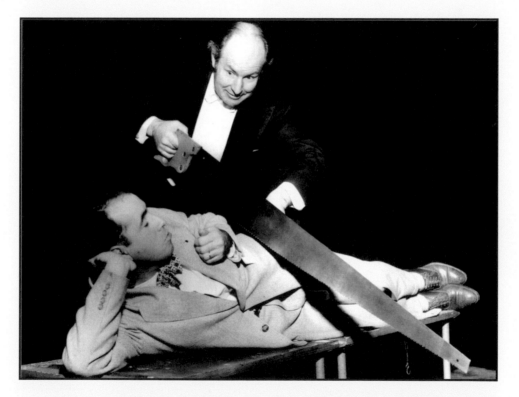

As a newspaperman in San Diego in 1950, Fleischman consents to being sawed in half.

In a few weeks, Fleischman went from being a copyboy, someone who runs errands, to being a journalist. He covered everything from flower shows to politics.

While Fleischman was working at the paper, his wife gave birth to their first child, Jane. Then the paper went out of business, and Fleischman was out of work.

Fleischman teamed up with a fellow reporter, and together they started their own weekly news publication called *Point*. When the magazine failed to make enough money to pay their salaries, Fleischman went back to writing fiction.

"That was the turning point," said Fleischman. "Once committed, I did nothing else but write novels. What really amazes me now," he added, "is that I had the confidence to take this huge risk that I would be able to make a living writing books."

In three months, Fleischman wrote and sold another adult novel, *The Man Who Died Laughing*. The editor changed the title of the book to *Shanghai Flame*, and it became a huge success.

"I was in Shanghai during the war," Fleischman

Book FACT

said, "so I wrote two or three novels set with Asian backgrounds."

In 1952, the Fleischmans' son, Paul, was born, and two years later, they had another daughter, Anne.

That same year, Fleischman published a new adult novel, entitled *Blood Alley*. The movie star John Wayne bought the film rights to *Blood Alley* and hired Fleischman to write the screenplay, the script for the movie. That led to a long-term contract for Fleischman to write more screenplays.

Now that he was earning a substantial salary, Fleischman and his family moved into a house near the

Cross-Pollination

Fleischman believes that the arts cross-pollinate, which means that an artist can transfer a skill or technique from one area to another.

I've learned a lot about writing novels from screenwriting and vice versa. It was my good fortune that the first screenplay I did was based on a novel of mine. The director was William A. Wellman. He had directed a movie called *Wings*. It was the first film to win an Academy Award, and Wellman really knew his storytelling stuff. I got a lot of tips from him. He said, "If we just take these two sentences apart, there's a scene in there," and he was right. I learned to open things up and see what's inside.

beach in Santa Monica, California, where he still lives.

Screenwriting helped Fleischman sharpen his writing skills. He learned how to develop strong scenes with dramatic endings and how to say the most with the least words. Then, just as Fleischman was to begin work on an original Western, the screenwriters went on strike in Hollywood. Fleischman was out of work again. However, his typewriter was not inactive for long. A new project was waiting in the wings, and he took a chance to write for an entirely different audience.

Mr. Mysterious

As children, Jane, Paul, and Anne Fleischman did not know much about their father's occupation. They knew that he worked at home and that he used a typewriter. Eleven-year-old Jane understood that her father wrote books, but it did not impress her. She was more interested in a visit by Leo Politi, a children's author, to the Santa Monica Public Library for a book signing.

Fleischman made a decision. He would take another chance. He would devote time to writing a children's book, and Jane, Paul, and Anne would be in it. The main character, of course, would be a magician. The book, *Mr. Mysterious and Company*, is about a family that travels across the Old West in a covered wagon. The characters use their common sense to outsmart the scoundrels who threaten them, and Fleischman uses a magic trick to resolve the story's ending. The book was published by the Atlantic Monthly Press in 1962.

When the screenwriters' strike ended, Fleischman returned to finish the script for the Western, which was called *The Deadly Companions*. He also formed his own film company with the actress Maureen O'Hara to produce the movie. Unfortunately, it was not a box office success.

In the meantime, reviews of *Mr. Mysterious and Company* were glowing. Fan mail from young readers all over the country poured in, as did invitations for Fleischman to speak at schools and libraries. It was not long before he found himself signing autographs at a library in Santa Monica. Anne, seven years old, was among his enthusiastic admirers.

Inspired by the days that he and Buddy Ryan traveled through the rugged Sierra Nevada mountains, Fleischman wrote his next children's book, *By the Great Horn Spoon!*, which was later made into a movie entitled *Bullwhip Griffin*. The book was set during California's gold rush in the mid-1800s, when hundreds of thousands of people journeyed to California with hopes of discovering gold in the mountains and riverbeds.

"I am fascinated by the old gold rush period," he said. "It's so rich and full of fun. There is so much humor in it. *By the Great Horn Spoon!* kept me laughing as I wrote each chapter."

Bandit's Moon and *The Giant Rat of Sumatra* were also set during this era. All three novels required a lot of research.

"I don't like dates," Fleischman said, "but I do like history because history is storytelling. I can lose myself in a historical period." He prepares a

Fleischman poses with his family on a movie set. His wife Betty is on the left; Fleischman is holding Anne, while Jane and Paul stand in front of him.

research notebook for each novel he writes. "I am very accurate," he said. "I don't have the patience to sit down and read forty books and then write. No, I begin the story, continuing the research as I write."

Sid Fleischman has written over fifty-two books for children. He said ideas are lurking everywhere. Sometimes they are in strange folk beliefs, like the fear of the number thirteen, which became the basis for his time travel novel, *The 13th Floor*. *The Ghost in the Noonday Sun* began with a superstitious belief that a person born at the stroke of midnight will have the power to see spirits.

Chancy and the Grand Rascal was the first book Fleischman wrote that was a tall tale. It was also where he introduced a midwestern farmer named McBroom, who later became the main character in his popular and very funny series of McBroom yarns.

Fleischman's experiences as a vaudeville magician play a part in *Jim Ugly*, *The Entertainer and the Dybbuk*, and *The Ghost in the Noonday Sun*. His work as a newspaperman comes to life in *Humbug Mountain*.

Many of Fleischman's main characters are young people who are on a quest and who take chances in fighting opposing forces. Ultimately they grow and change, like Jack in *By the Great Horn Spoon!* and Jemmy and Prince Brat in *The Whipping Boy.*

At one time Fleischman said that he would not write nonfiction, but that changed when he became interested in the life of the great magician and illusionist Harry Houdini. When he was alive, Houdini was as famous as anybody in the world. Everybody knew him, the man who could escape from jails, handcuffs, straightjackets—anything. He made headlines around the world. When Fleischman was working on Houdini's biography, he asked kids in schools if they had ever heard of Houdini. Every hand went up. Fleischman said, "That's phenomenal—after he'd been dead

The world's most famous magician, Harry Houdini. Fleischman's book *Escape! The Story of the Great Houdini* has been highly praised.

for eighty years." In 1935, about ten years after Houdini's death, Fleischman met Bess, Houdini's widow. She gave him photographs of Houdini that Fleischman used in *Escape! The Story of the Great Houdini*, a biography of the illusionist.

Fleischman went back to writing fiction with a trickster tale set in the country of Siam, today known as Thailand.

> I have often used animals as supporting players in my novels. The pig in *By the Great Horn Spoon!*, for example, and the half wolf, half dog in *Jim Ugly*. In *The White Elephant*, I not only returned to the Far East for a story but cast an animal in a lead role—the rare white elephant.

Fleischman drew on his Jewish heritage and combined it with his passion for magic and his flair for humor in his most recent novel, *The Entertainer and the Dybbuk*. A dybbuk is a type of ghost in Jewish folklore, a wandering soul that can possess the body of a living person. He said:

> I felt this to be the most personal novel I was ever moved to write. I was long affected by the complete loss of all my father's aunts, uncles, and

cousins, who had remained behind in Ukraine when the Nazis came through during the Second World War, murdering whole villages of Jews as they went. I used my father's village, Olyk, as the setting where the boy who became the dybbuk of the title was murdered. In the novel, he has returned to find the German officer who shot him full of holes. I used my own Jewish first name for the boy dybbuk, Avrom.

Book FACT

The Sid Fleischman Humor Award

Fleischman is a longtime member and friend of the Society of Children's Book Writers and Illustrators, an organization for people involved in writing, illustrating, and publishing books for young readers.

When the Society of Children's Book Writers and Illustrators asked me if they might name a humor award after me, I suggested they wait until I was dead. They couldn't wait that long and honored me at once. I am, of course, delighted.

Fleischman received the first award in 2002.

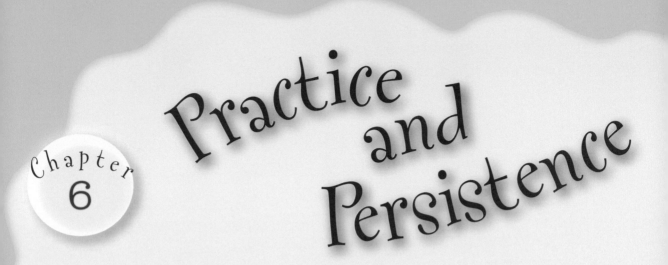

Chapter 6

Practice and Persistence

Fleischman saw similarities between writing and doing magic very early on in his career. He said:

> I saw certain types of short stories as literary magic tricks. That was a big revelation to me. It gave me confidence. I knew what made magic tricks work, so it was just a matter of adjusting my skills to the demands of storytelling.

On the other hand, Fleischman learned how complex writing could be.

> You're developing characters and scenes. You're developing relationships. You're developing plot

and filling in background.
You're discovering how people
talk and how they react,
all of these things at once.
It's a juggling trick. It does
take a lot of skill. I'm still
learning.

Fleischman tries to
make the final draft of his
stories as close to perfect
as he can.

"I think most writers
do," he said. "I have to
rewrite all the time. I always feel
there's a better way of saying
something, a fresher way."

One of Fleischman's
research notebooks
is labeled "Great
Unnamed Novel."

Fleischman rewrites each page
as he goes along.

"I stay on a page for a week, if I must. I enjoy
the process. Of course, when I finish and get a
page that I really like, that's the great reward. It's
the satisfaction of doing things really well."

Fleischman considers himself a perfectionist, but
he did not start out that way. In his early days as a

writer, he worked very quickly. Now he does not. He said:

> The reader doesn't care how long it took you to write a book. I take as much time as I need. I don't shove problems aside to be worked out later. If I have a problem I solve it right then. When I reach the last page of a novel, it's finished.

Fleischman works at a big wooden table in a paneled room that he uses as an office. The room overlooks a patio where he grows Babcock peaches, Japanese pears, oranges, and limes. He starts his

Fleischman enjoys working in his garden, which is full of flowers and fruit trees.

Book FACT

Award-Winning Books

Sid Fleischman's books have won many awards. Here are just a few of them:

By the Great Horn Spoon!
- Boys Club of America Junior Book Award
- Southern California Council on Literature for Children and Young People Award
- Western Writers of America Spur Award

Escape! The Story of the Great Houdini
- Boston Globe–Horn Book Honor Book
- American Library Association Notable Children's Book
- American Library Association Best Book for Young Adults

Humbug Mountain
- The Boston Globe/Horn Book Award
- National Book Award Finalist
- School Library Journal Best of the Best Books
- Indiana Young Hoosier Book Award

Jingo Django
- American Library Association Notable Book

Mr. Mysterious and Company
- The Boston Globe/Horn Book Award

The Scarebird
- Horn Book Fanfare
- The Paul A. Witty Award
- Parenting's Reading Magic Award
- Redbook's Children's Picture Books Award

The 13th Floor: A Ghost Story
- 1995 Society of School Librarians International Book Award
- Arkansas Charlie May Simon Children's Book Award
- California Young Reader Medal
- Maryland Black-Eyed Susan Book Award

The Whipping Boy
- Newbery Medal
- Arkansas Charlie May Simon Children's Book Award
- Hawaii Nene Award
- Wisconsin Golden Archer Award

Sid Fleischman has not lost his skill with magic— but now he uses it to write books as well.

writing day with some orange juice, and then he heads for his office. Generally, he works for an hour or two and then stops for breakfast and a shower. He quickly gets back to his desk. If he is working on the difficult beginning pages of a novel, he is worn out by noon and quits for the day and takes a nap. Once the novel is well launched, he spends a few more hours writing in the afternoon. When the book is nearly complete, Fleischman works steadily, morning, afternoon, and evening, until it is finished.

In *The Abracadabra Kid: A Writer's Life*, Fleischman's autobiography, he offers these pointers to aspiring writers:

- Let your main character solve the story problem. Let him or her be changed by the events in the story.

- Avoid making a rock or chair or other inanimate object be the hero of your story. Write about living things.

- Tease out dramatic moments.

- Fully develop important scenes; keep trivial scenes brief.

- Give weather reports to give a sense of reality to scenes.

- Use fresh, vivid images.

- Strong villains make strong heroes. Allow important characters to make grand entrances, if you can.

- If there is a plot hole in your story, point it out to the reader and the hole will vanish like magic.

Father-Son Newberys

Sid Fleischman's son, Paul, is also a writer—a poet, playwright, and children's author. His books include such award-winners as *Seedfolks*, *Whirligig*, *Graven Images*, and *Seek*. In 1989, two years after Fleischman won the Newbery Medal for *The Whipping Boy*, Paul won the Newbery for his book *Joyful Noise*.

"The whole family was thrilled. It was lightning striking twice," Sid Fleischman said. "Now, people get us mixed up, thinking I wrote one of his novels or that he wrote one of mine."

43

Fleischman with two of his grandchildren on a California beach. Sid Fleischman has been showing children wonderful things for his whole career.

Fleischman said he never gives people the advice they expect to get when they ask him about how to become a writer. He said:

Other authors may say you have to read a lot and keep diaries. That's true, but what you have to have is persistence and confidence in yourself. And you've got to work at both. You've got to practice. Writing has to be practiced. It's like learning a musical instrument or anything else. Those are the real secrets, it seems to me—practice and persistence. The two Ps.

Selected Books by Sid Fleischman

- The Abracadabra Kid: A Writer's Life
- Bandit's Moon
- The Bloodhound Gang in the Case of Princess Tomorrow
- The Bloodhound Gang in the Case of the 264-Pound Burglar
- The Bloodhound Gang in the Case of the Cackling Ghost
- The Bloodhound Gang in the Case of the Flying Clock
- The Bloodhound Gang in the Case of the Secret Message
- Bo and Mzzz Mad
- By the Great Horn Spoon!
- A Carnival of Animals
- Chancy and the Grand Rascal
- Disappearing Act
- The Entertainer and the Dybbuk
- Escape! The Story of the Great Houdini
- The Ghost in the Noonday Sun
- The Ghost on Saturday Night
- The Giant Rat of Sumatra: Or Pirates Galore
- Here Comes McBroom: Three More Tall Tales
- The Hey Hey Man
- Humbug Mountain
- Jim Bridger's Alarm Clock
- Jim Ugly
- Jingo Django
- Longbeard the Wizard
- McBroom and the Big Race
- McBroom and the Big Wind
- McBroom Tells a Lie
- McBroom Tells the Truth
- McBroom the Rainmaker
- McBroom's Almanac
- McBroom's Ear
- McBroom's Ghost
- McBroom's Wonderful One-Acre Farm
- McBroom's Zoo
- Me and the Man on the Moon-Eyed Horse
- The Midnight Horse
- Mr. Mysterious and Company
- Mr. Mysterious's Secrets of Magic
- The Scarebird
- The 13th Floor: A Ghost Story
- The Whipping Boy
- The White Elephant
- The Wooden Cat Man

conjurer (CON-jer-er)—An entertainer who performs magic tricks.

dybbuk (DIB-ik)—A type of ghost in Jewish folklore; a wandering soul that can possess the body of a living person.

immigrant—A person who goes to another country and settles there.

mirthful—Full of good humor.

nirvana (nur-VAH-na)—A place of total happiness; heaven.

sharpshooter—Someone who shoots a gun with precision.

sweatshop—A crowded workplace with poor conditions where the workers are overworked and underpaid.

tuition—A fee for going to a school or college.

vaudeville (VOD-vil)—Entertainment that was popular in the late 1800s and early 1900s, including singers, dancers, comics, and magicians.

ventriloquist (ven-TRIL-a-quist)—Someone who performs with a dummy, making it look as if the dummy is speaking.

Books

Bull, Jane. *The Magic Book*. New York: DK Publishing, 2002.

Fleischman, Sid. *The Abracadabra Kid: A Writer's Life*. New York: HarperTrophy, 1998.

Freedman, Jeri. *Sid Fleischman*. New York: Rosen, 2004.

Ho, Oliver. *Young Magician: Magic Tricks*. New York: Sterling Publishing, 2003.

Ruffin, Frances. *Meet Sid Fleischman*. New York: PowerKids Press, 2006.

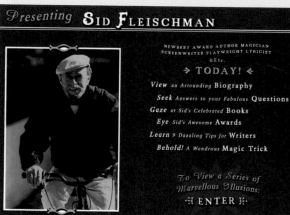

Internet Addresses

Sid Fleischman:
Official Site
<http://www.sidfleischman.com/>

The Author Corner: Sid Fleischman
<http://www.carr.org/authco/fleischman.htm>

Index

A
Adams, John, 25

B
books by Sid Fleischman
  Bandit's Moon, 33
  Between Cocktails, 21–22
  Blood Alley, 29
  By the Great Horn Spoon!
    33, 35, 36, 41
  *Chancy and the Grand
    Rascal*, 34
  *The Entertainer and the
    Dybbuk*, 34, 36–37
  *Escape! The Story of the
    Great Houdini*,
    35–36, 41
  *The Ghost in the
    Noonday Sun*, 34
  *The Giant Rat of
    Sumatra*, 33
  Humbug Mountain, 34,
    41
  Jim Ugly, 11, 34, 36
  Jingo Django, 41
  *The Man Who Died
    Laughing (Shanghai
    Flame)*, 28
  *Mr. Mysterious and
    Company*, 31–32, 41
  The Scarebird, 41

  *The Straw Donkey
    Case*, 26
  *The 13th Floor: A Ghost
    Story*, 34, 41
  The Whipping Boy,
    5–7, 35, 41, 43
  The White Elephant, 36
Brindle, Max, 7
Bullwhip Griffin, 33

F
Fait, Charles W. (Professor
  Fait the Great), 18–19
Fleischman, Anne, 29, 31
Fleischman, Arleen, 9
Fleischman, Betty
  (Taylor), 5, 25
Fleischman, Jane, 28, 31
Fleischman, Paul, 29,
  31, 43
Fleischman, Pearl, 9
Fleischman, Reuben,
  8–11, 14, 15, 16–17
Fleischman, Sadie, 8–9,
  10, 16
Fleischman, Sid (Albert
  Sidney; Avrom Zalmon)
  awards, 5, 37, 41
  childhood, 8–12, 13–20
  education, 20, 21, 23,
    24–25
  magic career, 15–17,
    18–22, 23–24
  military experiences,
    25–26

  writing career, 21–23,
    24–25, 26, 27–37
  writing methods and
    advice, 38–40,
    42–44

H
Houdini, Harry, 35–36

L
Little Shop of Hocus
  Pocus, 23–24

M
The Mirthful Conjurers,
  20–21, 24

N
Newbery Medal, 5, 41, 43

P
Point, 28
Politi, Leo, 31

R
Ryan, Buddy, 20, 32

S
San Diego Daily Journal,
  27–28
San Diego State College,
  24
See'n Is Believ'n, 20–21,
  24

V
vaudeville, 21

W
Wayne, John, 29
World War II, 25, 26, 28

J B FLEISCHMAN
Parker-Rock, Michelle.
Sid Fleischman :an
 author kids love /
R0111498982   SDY_SP

SANDY SPRINGS

ATLANTA-FULTON COUNTY LIBRARY